SandCastle

Let's Go!

LET'S GO

BY

BOAT

ANDERS HANSON

Consulting Editor, Diane Craig, M.A./Reading Specialist

ABDO Publishing Company

Published by ABDO Publishing Company, 8000 West 78th Street, Edina, MN 55439

Copyright © 2008 by Abdo Consulting Group, Inc. International copyrights reserved in all countries. No part of this book may be reproduced in any form without written permission from the publisher. SandCastle™ is a trademark and logo of ABDO Publishing Company.

Printed in the United States.

Editor: Pam Price
Curriculum Coordinator: Nancy Tuminelly
Cover and Interior Design and Production: Mighty Media
Photo Credits: Shutterstock

Library of Congress Cataloging-in-Publication Data

Hanson, Anders, 1980-
Let's go by boat / Anders Hanson.
p. cm. -- (Let's go!)
ISBN 978-1-59928-894-9
1. Boats and boating--Juvenile literature. I. Title.

VM150.H28 2007
797.1--dc22

2007006656

SandCastle™ Level: Transitional

SandCastle™ books are created by a team of professional educators, reading specialists, and content developers around five essential components--phonemic awareness, phonics, vocabulary, text comprehension, and fluency--to assist young readers as they develop reading skills and increase their general knowledge. All books are written, reviewed, and leveled for guided reading, early intervention reading, and Accelerated Reader® programs for use in shared, guided, and independent reading and writing activities to support a balanced approach to literacy instruction. The SandCastle™ series has four levels that correspond to early literacy development. The levels are provided to help teachers and parents select appropriate books for young readers.

Emerging Readers
(no flags)

Beginning Readers
(1 flag)

Transitional Readers
(2 flags)

Fluent Readers
(3 flags)

SandCastle™ would like to hear from you. Please send us your comments or questions.

sandcastle@abdopublishing.com

Boats float! Boats are vessels that carry people and cargo over water.

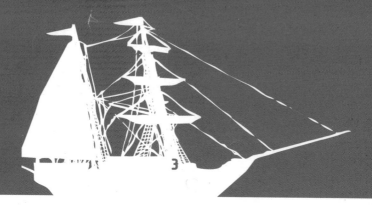

3

The top of a boat is called the deck.

A steering wheel turns the boat.

A propeller can make a motorboat go forward or backward.

Sails move sailboats with wind power.

Tracy paddles a canoe on a lake.

Erik likes to watch
the crew unload
the ferry.

Ted jumps off
a boat to go
scuba diving.

18

Dan always wears
a life vest when
he is in a boat or
around water.

HAVE YOU BEEN IN A BOAT?

WHERE DID YOU GO?

canoe

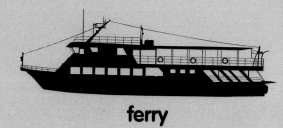

ferry

fishing boat

motorboat

sailboat

Ancient Egyptians made wooden boats held together with pegs.

Large watercraft are called ships, not boats. In general, a boat can fit on a ship, but a ship cannot fit on a boat.

In 1978, Ken Warby set a world record by going 317 miles per hour in his jet-powered boat.

GLOSSARY

paddle – to move a boat through water using a device with a thin handle and a wide, flat blade at one or both ends.

propeller – a device with blades used to move a vehicle such as an airplane or a boat.

scuba dive – to swim underwater while breathing from a tank of air.

vessel – a large boat or ship.

watercraft – a ship or boat.

To see a complete list of SandCastle™ books and other nonfiction titles from ABDO Publishing Company, visit **www.abdopublishing.com**.

8000 West 78th Street, Edina, MN 55439 • 800-800-1312 • 952-831-1632 fax